JOE KELLY'S
GREATEST EVER LITTLE
TRIVIA BOOK

or
Just Because It's Trivia Doesn't Mean It Isn't Important

By JOE KELLY

Good Times Publishing Company
P. O. Box 4545
Utica, NY 13504

Printed in Yorkville, N.Y. by Vicks Lithograph &
Printing Corporation

PREFACE

Q. Why was this book written?

A. I had to do something with all the scraps of information I've hoarded for all these years.

Q. Who was this book written for?

A. Everybody who loves the Utica area, from near or from afar.

Q. Will I like this book?

A. Only if you're interested in the Utica area, its people, its institutions, its history, and want to impress friends with your trivia knowledge. Heck, you might even win a bet or two.

Q. What should I keep in mind while reading this book?

A. Just because it's trivia doesn't mean it isn't important.

DEDICATION

Q. Who are Jackie Serley and Cindy Miner?

A. They are my daughters and this book is dedicated to them.

TABLE OF CONTENTS

ACKNOWLEDGMENTS

Q. Who are the people who helped me put this book together?

A. In one way or another, help was provided by Frank Tomaino, Dave Dudajek, Randall Kimberly, Barbara Charzuk, of the Observer-Dispatch; Utica Public Library staffers, especially Darby O'Brien; folks at the Oneida County Historical Society, especially Douglas Preston; the cooperative people at Vicks Lithograph & Printing, especially Dana Jerrard; generations of Utica newspaper reporters and authors whose articles and books were read in order to find the answers to the questions; and Kathy Kelly, my wife, whose support and hard work made this book happen.

Q. If all of the above mentioned people were with me right now, what would I say?

A. Thank you, thank you very much.

FIRST THINGS FIRST

CHAPTER ONE

Q. What was the first name given to the area in which Utica would eventually be built?

A. Unundadages, which is Iroquois for "around the hill."

Q. What was the first name given to Unundadages by white settlers?

A. Old Fort Schuyler, which became the Village of Utica in 1798.

Q. Who was Utica's first postmaster?

A. John Post, a merchant, was appointed postmaster in 1793.

Q. Where was the first school in Old Fort Schuyler?

A. On Main Street between First and Second streets, built in 1797.

Q. Who was the first white man to own the land on which Utica was to be built?

A. William Cosby, an unscrupulous English governor appointed by King George II.

Q. Who were Utica's first merchants?

A. In 1789, Peter Smith opened a small trading post in an area later known as Bagg's Square, and he was quickly followed by John Post.

Q. What do Christian Reall, Marcus Damuth and George Weaver have in common?

A. They and their families were this area's first white settlers.

Q. Where did they build their first cabins?

A. In an area that is now north Utica.

Q. Who first surveyed what later became Utica?

A. John Bleecker in 1786.

Q. Who was the area's first physician?

A. Dr. Francis Guiteau, who came to Old Fort Schuyler in 1792.

Q. Who built Utica's first frame house?

A. John Post, who arrived by boat on the Mohawk River in 1790.

Q. What was the name of Utica's first hotel?

A. Bagg's Hotel, which opened for business at John and Main Streets in 1794.

Q. Which Utica street was the first to be paved?

A. A small section of Genesee Street, near Whitesboro Street, was paved with cobblestones around 1800.

Q. Which street was the first to be paved with asphalt?

A. Rutger Street in 1886.

Q. Who wrote the first history of Oneida County?

A. Pomroy Jones of Westmoreland wrote "Annals and Recollections of Oneida County" in the 1850s.

Q. What happened in 1805 to improve fire protection?

A. Utica purchased its first hand pumper, which replaced bucket brigades.

Q. What happened in 1864 to further improve Utica fire protection?

A. The first horse-drawn steam engine was purchased.

Q. What happened in 1913 to again improve Utica's fire protection?

A. The first motorized fire engine was purchased.

Q. Who was the first president of the Village of Utica?

A. Talcott Camp, 1798.

Q. Who was the first mayor of the City of Utica?

A. Joseph Kirkland, 1832.

Q. When did regular mail service first begin and who was the letter carrier?

A. In 1793, Simeon Pool had a route from Canajoharie through Utica to Whitestown.

Q. What was Utica's first bank?

A. A branch office of the Manhattan Bank of New York City did business on the west corner of Hotel and Whitesboro streets starting in 1809.

Q. What signer of the Declaration of Independence was on the Manhattan branch bank's first board of directors?

A. William Floyd.

Q. What Utica store was the first to be lighted by electricity?

A. The Buckley-Meyers Dry Goods Store, on the east side of Genesee Street between Elizabeth and Devereux, in 1883.

Q. What was the first institution to be completely wired for electricity?

A. Masonic Home, 1891.

Q. When was the first bridge built across the Mohawk River in this area?

A. In 1792, a crude bridge was built across the river in line with today's Second Street, but the flimsy structure washed away in less than a year.

Q. When was the first permanent bridge built across the Mohawk River on Genesee Street?

A. In 1797, a $400 bridge, paid for with proceeds from a lottery, was built.

Q. Who made Utica's first telephone call?

A. On Jan. 18, 1878, George Young telephoned from his house on Rutger Street to his bakery on Bleecker Street.

Q. When and where was the first Roman Catholic Mass celebrated in Utica?

A. In 1813 at John Devereux's home, northeast corner of Broad and Second streets.

Q. What was the name and location of Utica's first vaudeville theater?

A. In 1893, the Wonderland theater opened in Mechanics Hall, still standing at the northwest corner of Hotel and Liberty (Oriskany) streets.

Q. Who owned the first automobile in Utica?

A. In 1899, George Sanborn drove around town in a steam-powered car.

Q. Who was the first president of the Village of Whitesboro and president of the village's first bank?

A. Simon Dexter, born in Rhode Island in 1785, held both jobs.

Q. Who was the first president of the Utica Chamber of Commerce?

A. George Dunham, editor of The Utica Daily Press, was president, 1896-98.

Q. Who developed Utica's first street railway and the state's first telegraph company?

A. John Butterfield, founder of the Overland Mail, the country's first transcontinental stagecoach line.

Q. Who was the first Oneida County judge?

A. Jedediah Sanger, 1798, founder of New Hartford.

Q. When were the first traffic lights installed on Utica streets?

A. June 11, 1926.

Q. When Utica was incorporated as a city in 1832, what was one of the first laws to be adopted?

A. It was against the law to buy anything on Sunday except milk.

Q. What was Utica's first speed limit?

A. It was illegal to "ride or drive any horse or horses in any of the streets of the said city faster than a moderate trot."

Q. What were Utica's first police officers called?

A. The Night Watch.

Q. When did Utica get its first full-time police department?

A. In 1862, a police force of 12 officers was hired.

Q. Who was Utica's first chief of police?

A. David Hess.

Q. Who was this area's first state senator?

A. Thomas Gold of Whitesboro, 1796-1802.

Q. What was the American Journal of Insanity?

A. Published by the New York State Lunatic Asylum, which opened in Utica in 1843, it was the first journal in the world devoted to the treatment of mental illness.

Q. What was Utica's first fraternal or service organization?

A. Utica Lodge No. 47, F. & A. M., which, as of 1993, has provided 177 years of Masonic service.

Q. When were Utica's first parking meters installed?

A. Six hundred parking meters were put into service in July, 1940.

Q. In what year did the Utica Police Department first start using patrol cars?

A. 1933.

Q. When did Utica first get air mail service?

A. June 1, 1928.

Q. What was F.W. Woolworth's connection to Utica?

A. He opened his first store in downtown Utica's Arcade Building on Genesee Street in 1879.

Q. Why did Woolworth call his first store "The Great Five Cent Store"?

A. Every item in the store sold for five cents.

Q. What was the first item sold by Woolworth in his first store?

A. A five-cent coal shovel.

Q. Who was the first Oneida County executive?

A. Charles Lanigan, elected in 1962.

Q. Who was the first Italian to settle in Utica?

A. Dr. John Marchisi, a druggist and fireworks manufacturer, arrived in 1815.

Q. When were voting machines first used in Utica?

A. Two machines were used in 1898 as an experiment, and 28 more machines were added the next year.

Q. Where was New York State's first cotton mill?

A. It opened in 1809 in New York Mills.

Q. Where was New York State's first woolen mill?

A. It was built near Oriskany in 1811.

Q. Where was Utica's first brewery?

A. William Inman, father of the famous painter Henry Inman, brewed beer at the corner of Broadway and Whitesboro streets starting about 1804.

GEOGRAPHY DOESN'T HAVE TO BE BORING

CHAPTER TWO

Q. How many Uticas are there in the United States?

A. 19.

Q. In what states are Uticas located?

A. New York, Mississippi, Pennsylvania, Ohio, Indiana, Illinois, Michigan, Wisconsin, Minnesota, Montana, South Dakota, Nebraska, Iowa, Kansas, Missouri, Oklahoma, Kentucky, Maryland, Alaska.

Q. What do all those Uticas have in common?

A. All are named after Utica, N.Y.

Q. Which Utica is the most populated?

A. Utica, N.Y.

Q. Which is the second most populated?

A. Utica, Michigan.

Q. Which is the smallest Utica?

A. Utica, Alaska, has a population of one, a hermit who lives in the woods.

Q. Where did the name Utica come from?

A. Utica, N.Y., is named after Utica, Tunisia, once a great seaport on North Africa's Mediterranean coast.

Q. What size is the Utica in Tunisia today?

A. It has fewer than 100 homes and a few shops.

Q. How do the Uticans in Tunisia pronounce their community's name?

A. U Tee Ca.

Q. Are there Uticas in any other countries?

A. There is a Utica in Wales and Canada.

Q. What are the six towns whose borders touch Utica's city line?

A. Deerfield, Schuyler, Frankfort, New Hartford, Whitestown and Marcy.

Q. What is the area of Oneida County?

A. 727,077 acres.

Q. What Oneida County town has the biggest area?

A. The Town of Forestport, 46,386 acres.

Q. What Oneida County town has the smallest area?

A. The Town of New Hartford, 13,303 acres.

Q. What is Utica's area?

A. 10,387 acres.

Q. When Utica became a city in 1832, what were the only other cities in New York State?

A. New York, Albany, Troy, Hudson and Schenectady.

Q. Oneida County and the state of Rhode Island have what in common?

A. They are practically the same size.

Q. What do Utica, New York, and Rome, New York, have in common with Utica, Kentucky, and Rome, Kentucky?

A. The Utica and Rome in New York are about 12 miles apart and the Utica and Rome in Kentucky are about 12 miles apart.

Q. What waterways does Genesee Street cross?

A. The Mohawk River, the Erie Canal, Realls Creek and Sauquoit Creek.

Q. What happened to Pearl Street, which once ran east and west between Genesee Street and Broadway?

A. It was eliminated to make room for what is now the Radisson Hotel and the city's parking garage.

Q. What seldom-used street runs east and west behind the Children's Museum and under the Genesee Street bridge?

A. Water Street.

Q. Why is Cornhill so named?

A. Because of immense corn fields that once grew along South Street, east of Steuben Street.

Q. When and why was the course of the Mohawk River through Utica changed?

A. A contract to divert the river, thus preventing flooding in the Bagg's Square area, was awarded in 1907.

Q. How big is the Utica Marsh?

A. Located off Barnes Avenue, there are 210 acres.

Q. The elevation of Genesee Street, at the intersection with Lafayette and Bleecker streets, is how high above sea level?

A. 436 feet.

Q. Oneida County Airport is how many feet above sea level?

A. 743 feet.

Q. In 1839, what was the southern border of Utica?

A. Rutger Street, and there were only five houses on its southern side.

Q. How many acres of parks are within Utica's city limits?

A. More than 1,000.

Q. What is the most romantic intersection in Utica?

A. Where JOHN meets ELIZABETH and PARK.

Q. Where exactly was Old Fort Schuyler?

A. In an area bounded today by Main Street, Second Street and Third Avenue and the railroad tracks.

Q. What are the names of the two Proctor parks?

A. Frederick T. Proctor Park is the one farthest north on Culver Avenue and Thomas R. Proctor Park is to the south.

THAT'S ENTERTAINMENT

CHAPTER   THREE

Q. What ex-Utican's show business career started as a member of Walt Disney's Mickey Mouse Club?

A. Annette Funicello was one of the original Mouseketeers, starting in October, 1955.

Q. How old is Annette?

A. She was born Oct. 22, 1942.

Q. What television series did Annette star in?

A. "Spin and Marty" and "Adventures in Dairyland," and she guest starred on the "Danny Thomas Show" and "Zorro."

Q. What were her three top songs?

A. "Tall Paul," "How Will I Know My Love," and "Dio Mio."

Q. Why did many Uticans get mad at Annette?

A. In a 1983 song she referred to Utica as "Sin City of the East," something she later apologized for.

Q. In what movie did she make her motion picture debut?

A. Walt Disney's hit comedy, "The Shaggy Dog," starring Fred MacMurray.

Q. What beach party movies did Annette star in?

A. Along with beach buddy Frankie Avalon, she starred in "Beach Blanket Bingo," "Muscle Beach Party," "Bikini Beach" and "Beach Party."

Q. What movie did Annette star in with Fabian?

A. "Thunder Alley," 1967.

Q. What product did Annette promote in a long series of television commercials?

A. Skippy Peanut Butter.

Q. When was opening night at the Stanley Theater?

A. On Sept. 9, 1928, a standing-room-only crowd watched "Ramona," a silent movie.

Q. What was special about the Stanley's orchestra pit?

A. It was one of the first elevated orchestra pits in the country.

Q. What Utican became a world-famous writer?

A. The late John D. MacDonald.

Q. What famous character did MacDonald create?

A. Travis McGee.

Q. Where in Utica did MacDonald live?

A. State Street, just below Oneida Square.

Q. While struggling to make it as a writer, what did MacDonald do to make a living?

A. He was executive secretary of the Taxpayers Research Bureau at Utica City Hall.

Q. Where did MacDonald go to elementary school and high school?

A. John F. Hughes and Utica Free Academy, class of 1933.

Q. Where did MacDonald work part time during his school years?

A. He was a caddy at Valley View Golf Course.

Q. Where did MacDonald go to college?

A. Syracuse University, and then to Harvard for a master's degree in business administration.

Q. What did MacDonald do during World War II?

A. He was an Army officer with the Office of Strategic Services, forerunner of the Central Intelligence Agency.

Q. What was MacDonald paid for his first published short story, written during the war?

A. $25.

Q. After moving from Utica, where did MacDonald spend his summers?

A. At his Piseco Lake camp in the Adirondacks.

Q. Where did he spend his winters?

A. In Florida.

Q. Who is known as Utica's Elvis?

A. Joe Angerosa, who for many years has performed his "Memories of Elvis" show.

Q. What Utica intersection once had three movie theaters?

A. The Olympic, Avon and Utica theaters were once at the intersection of Lafayette and Washington streets.

Q. The Olympic was built on the site of what theater?

A. The Hippodrome Theater.

Q. What items were given to moviegoers at east Utica's Rialto Theater?

A. Dishware.

Q. Who is Ronnie Zito?

A. Zito, who grew up on Seymour Avenue between Rutger and South, was singer Bobby Darin's drummer.

Q. What author, actor, newspaper columnist, television performer, and radio personality called Utica his adopted home?

A. Ken Murray, who was most famous for his home movies of the movie stars.

Q. Who was the Big D?

A. Nick Dardano, a popular 1960's disc jockey.

Q. What is the name of the roller coaster at the Sylvan Beach Amuesment Park?

A. The Galaxi.

Q. Where did Dick Clark, of American Bandstand fame, get his start in the entertainment business?

A. While waiting to begin his first year at Syracuse University in 1947, the 17-year-old got a job at Utica radio station WRUN doing the weather, station breaks and news.

Q. What was Dick Clark's first job in television?

A. After graduating from college he got a broadcasting job at WKTV.

Q. What on-air name did Dick Clark use while at WKTV?

A. Dick Clay.

Q. What was Dick Clark's salary at WKTV?

A. $52.50 a week.

Q. Dick Clark is how old?

A. He was born November 30, 1929.

Q. What long-time Utica radio personality once served on the Utica Board of Education, is a commercial pilot, motorcycle enthusiast, sign language instructor, Kentucky "colonel" and once had his own show on WKTV?

A. Danny Fusco.

Q. Where was the Lyric Theater?

A. On Varick Street in a building later occupied by the Utica Glass Works.

Q. What was Twist-A-Rama USA?

A. Utica's version of American Bandstand.

Q. Who hosted Twist-A-Rama USA?

A. Hank Brown, a long-time radio personality.

Q. When Utica was a regular stop for the Ringling Brothers, and Barnum & Bailey Circus, where did they set up the tents?

A. In a field now occupied by the North Utica Shopping Center.

Q. What do Brad Clay, Craig Worthing, Jay Bortz, Buck Buckley, Tom Coyne, Ken Moore, Bill Fowler, John Swann and Danny Clinkscale all have in common?

A. At one time or another, all were hosts of "At Your Service," a WIBX radio talk show.

Q. Where was the Orpheum Theater located?

A. On the southeast corner of South and Miller streets.

Q. What national distinction belongs to the "Players of Utica?"

A. Formed in 1919, the theater group is the second oldest of its kind in the country.

Q. What long-time Utica politician once had a radio career?

A. In the 1940s and '50s, Lou Barile was an announcer on radio stations WIBX and WKAL.

Q. What was Ralph Romano noted for?

A. In the 1970s, he hosted a controversial talk show on radio station WBVM.

Q. Where in Utica were scenes of the Paul Newman movie "Slapshot" filmed?

A. At the Utica Memorial Auditorium.

Q. Why did Elvis Presley once stop in Utica?

A. On his way to Philadelphia for a concert in 1957, Elvis, who was driving his own car, stopped at the North Genesee Club Diner for breakfast on April 4.

Q. Where was the North Genesee Club Diner?

A. Southwest corner of Genesee Street and Riverside Drive, now the site of a gas station.

Q. What kind of car was Elvis driving?

A. A 1957 Cadillac, pink and black.

Q. When was Elvis supposed to have returned to Utica?

A. He was scheduled to give a concert at the Utica Memorial Auditorium on Aug. 19, 1977.

Q. What happened?

A. Presley died Aug. 16, 1977.

Q. How many people attended events at the Stanley Performing Arts Center in 1992?

A. More than 100,000.

Q. What connection does Alex Haley and his book "Roots" have with this area?

A. Haley started the book while teaching at Hamilton College in Clinton.

Q. What classic Revolutionary War novel was set in the Mohawk Valley?

A. "Drums Along the Mohawk" by Walter Edmonds.

Q. Who starred in the movie version of "Drums Along the Mohawk"?

A. Henry Fonda and Claudette Colbert.

Q. What are some other books by Walter Edmonds?

A. "Rome Haul", "Chad Hanna", "The Matchlock Gun", "Erie Water" and "Mostly Canallers."

Q. Where was Walter Edmonds born?

A. Hawkinsville, Town of Boonville, 1903.

SO WHERE DO ALL THOSE STREET NAMES COME FROM?

CHAPTER FOUR

Q. Taylor Avenue?

A. Lorenzo Taylor was city engineer from 1838 until 1850 and made many of Utica's early maps.

Q. Hubbell Street?

A. Matthew Hubbell came to Central New York in 1790 and bought land in what would become east Utica for $2.50 per acre.

Q. Hobart Street?

A. Bishop John Hobart was an Episcopal clergyman who did missionary work in Upstate New York in the early 1800s.

Q. Symonds Place?

A. Charles Symonds was president of the Utica City National Bank in the early 1900s, and president of the Oneida County Historical Society.

Q. Tilden Avenue?

A. Samuel Tilden was governor of New York, 1875-77.

Q. Dakin Street?

A. Samuel Dakin graduated from Hamilton College in 1821 and later became editor of the Utica Sentinel and Gazette.

Q. Schuyler Street?

A. Gen. Philip Schuyler was a Revolutionary War hero.

Q. Hopper Street?

A. James Hopper, a sea captain, came to Utica in 1801, bought land and became a merchant.

Q. Jay Street?

A. John Jay was the first chief justice of the United States, 1790 to 1795, resigning to become governor of New York.

Q. Mathews Avenue?

A. E.D. Mathews was a developer who built many homes in west Utica.

Q. Churchill Avenue?

A. E.D. Mathews had a wife and her maiden name was Churchill.

Q. McQuade Avenue?

A. Col. James McQuade was a Civil War hero and became Utica's mayor in 1870.

Q. Seymour Avenue?

A. Horatio Seymour was mayor of Utica, governor of New York and came within a whisker of defeating Ulysses S. Grant for president of the United States.

Q. Conkling Avenue?

A. Roscoe Conkling, a lawyer, was mayor of Utica, a congressman, U.S. Senator and close friend and adviser to President Grant.

Q. Varick Street?

A. Abraham Varick, a lawyer, settled in Utica in 1804 and for many years was an agent for the Holland Land Company, buying land for the company and for himself.

Q. Ann Street?

A. Named after Varick's wife, Ann.

Q. Dwyer Avenue?

A. James Dwyer was Utica's commissioner of Public Works in the early 1900s and owned much land in the area where Utica Boilers and CharlesTown now stand.

Q. Devereux Street?

A. Nicholas Devereux was an organizer of the Utica & Schenectady Railroad in 1827 and a founder of the Savings Bank of Utica.

Q. Hart Street?

A. Ephriam Hart was a merchant, iron manufacturer and a state senator, 1816-22.

Q. Erie Street?

A. The Erie Canal once ran parallel to the street.

Q. Grove Place?

A. DeWitt Grove was mayor of Utica, 1860-62.

Q. Ballantyne Brae and Bonnie Brae?

A. William Blaikie, president of the Savings Bank of Utica (1895-1909) moved here from

Scotland and gave streets running through his property names to remind him of home.

Q. Wetmore Street?

A. Edmund Wetmore was mayor of Utica, 1845, and later became president of the Savings Bank of Utica.

Q. Steuben Street?

A. Baron Von Steuben helped organize the American Army during the Revolutionary War.

Q. Gibson Road?

A. John Gibson was mayor of Utica in 1893.

Q. Herkimer Road?

A. General Nicholas Herkimer led his troops over this road on the way to Fort Stanwix, a march that resulted in the Revolutionary War's Battle of Oriskany.

Q. Dickinson Street?

A. Albert Dickinson was a reporter for the Utica Herald, a founder of The Daily Press and managing editor of the Saturday Globe.

Q. Kirkland Street?

A. Joseph Kirkland was mayor of Utica in 1832, the year the Village of Utica became the City of Utica.

Q. Cornelia Street?

A. Apollo Cooper, who moved to Old Fort Schuyler in 1790 and bought 117 acres in what became west Utica, had a daughter named Cornelia.

Q. Guelich Street?

A. Otto Guelich operated a wholesale butcher business in east Utica and subdivided his farm into building lots in the 1870s.

Q. Watson Place?

A. Dr. William Watson founded Utica Homeopathic Hospital in 1895, which changed its name to Memorial Hospital in 1927 and later merged with St. Luke's Hospital.

Q. Downer Avenue?

A. Charles Downer operated a lumberyard, first on Cooper Street and then on Lafayette Street, and supplied material to build many 19th century Utica homes.

Q. Morris Street?

A. Oneida County Judge Morris Miller, who was president of the Village of Utica in 1808, owned land where this street was laid out.

Q. Culver Avenue?

A. Utica native Abraham Culver, born in 1812, went to sea as a young man and earned enough money to open a wholesale grain business and freight forwarding operation.

Q. Sanger Avenue (New Hartford)?

A. Jedediah Sanger founded New Hartford in 1788, paying 50 cents an acre for 1,000 acres, which included the present day Village of New Hartford.

Q. Higby Road?

A. Joseph Higby, who arrived here not long after 1788, purchased 600 acres from Sanger and paid $1 per acre.

Q. Mather Avenue?

A. A.D. Mather operated a private bank in turn-of-the century Utica.

Q. Thieme Place?

A. In 1910, Robert Thieme and wife Barbara deeded to New Hartford a strip of land across their property for use as a street to be known as Thieme Place, a street which became part of Utica in the 1921 annexation.

Q. Sherman Place?

A. Utica's James Schoolcraft Sherman was vice president of the United States during the Taft administration.

Q. Saratoga Street?

A. Named after the Revolutionary War's Battle of Saratoga.

Q. Walker Street?

A. During the Revolutionary War, Col. Benjamin Walker, who is buried in Forest Hill Cemetery, was an aide to Gen. George Washington and Baron von Steuben at Valley Forge.

Q. Dunham Place?

A. George Dunham was editor of The Utica Daily Press from the late 1800s until the early 1900s.

Q. South Street?

A. It once marked Utica's southern boundary.

Q. Kossuth Avenue?

A. Lajos Kossuth, a Hungarian national hero who led a rebellion in his country in 1848, once visited Utica.

Q. Bacon Street?

A. Attorney William Bacon was a state assemblyman in 1850, State Supreme Court judge in 1853 and was elected to the U.S. Congress in 1876.

Q. Baker Avenue?

A. Frank Baker, a florist, was mayor of Utica, 1911-12.

Q. Geer Avenue?

A. Bert Geer was Utica's comptroller in the 1920s.

Q. Butterfield Avenue?

A. John Butterfield founded the Overland Mail stagecoach line, was president of the American Express Company, built a hotel, and in 1865 was elected Utica's mayor.

Q. Harriet Street?

A. John Butterfield's wife was named Harriet.

Q. Hammond Avenue?

A. The Rev. John Hammond was a preacher in Utica's pioneer days and he delivered his sermons in Bagg's Square.

Q. Stark Street?

A. Gen. John Stark defeated British and Hessian troops at the Battle of Bennington, 1777.

Q. Amy Avenue?

A. Named for Amy Perkins, whose family owned much land in south Utica.

Q. Brookline Drive, Sunnyside Drive, Dearborn Place, Ferndale Place, Brighton Place?

A. The developer who built homes on those streets conducted a contest and those were the winning names.

Q. Hollister Avenue?

A. Charles Merritt, a long-ago city engineer, named the street in honor of his mother, whose maiden name was Hollister.

Q. Beverly Place?

A. Named by the street's developer Orville Balch, who moved to Utica from Beverly, Mass.

Q. Poe Street?

A. Named after writer Edgar Allan Poe.

Q. Lincoln Avenue?

A. Every city has a street named after the president of the United States.

Q. Gilbert Street?

A. In the 1830s, Elisha Gilbert was a prominent Utica dry goods and leather goods dealer.

Q. Dawes Avenue?

A. Charles Dawes was vice president of the United States during the Coolidge administration.

Q. Derbyshire Place?

A. Miss Derbyshire was a housekeeper at Bagg's Hotel and the person most responsible for establishing the Utica Orphan Asylum.

Q. Plant Street?

A. Back when Utica was called Old Fort Schuyler, Benjamin Plant bought a farm near what is now Oneida Square.

Q. Talcott Road?

A. Charles Talcott of Utica was a U.S. congressman, 1911-15.

UTICA BOILERMAKER ROAD RACE

CHAPTER FIVE

Q. When was the first Boilermaker and how many runners registered to run?

A. Eight hundred runners signed up for the first race in 1978.

Q. How many runners signed up for the 1993 race?

A. Five thousand.

Q. What was the average age of male runners in the 1993 race?

A. 37.

Q. What was the average age of female runners in the 1993 race?

A. 33.

Q. Runners in the 1993 race came to Utica from how many states?

A. 39.

Q. How many runners finished the 1993 race?

A. 4,243.

Q. Who was 1993's winner?

A. Thomas Osano of Kenya.

Q. Who was 1993's female winner?

A. Gitte Karlshoj of Denmark.

Q. How long did it take for the winners to finish?

A. Osano finished in 43 minutes, 39 seconds; Karlshoj in 51 minutes, seven seconds.

Q. How long did it take the last runner to finish?

A. Virginia Sherman of Rome crossed the finish line in two hours, 17 minutes.

Q. What outstanding accomplishment was achieved by Joseph Kipsang of Kenya and Ena Guevaramora of Syracuse?

A. Both are two-time Boilermaker winners.

Q. What is the fastest Boilermaker ever run?

A. Thomas Osano, in 1993, and Sammy Lelei, in 1992, ran the course in identical times, 43 minutes, 39 seconds.

Q. What was the fastest Boilermaker ever run by a woman?

A. Jill Hunter of England finished the 1991 race in 48 minutes, 19 seconds.

Q. When is the Boilermaker run?

A. Always on the second Sunday in July.

Q. What was the starting time of the first Boilermaker?

A. 10:30 a.m., two hours later than it now starts.

Q. What designation has "Runner's World" magazine given the race?

A. The national magazine has selected the Boilermaker as one of the top 65 races in the country.

Q. What other national honor has the Boilermaker received?

A. It ranks second in the nation in "most community spirit," according to a "Runner's World" magazine contest.

Q. Who is the director of the Boilermaker?

A. Earle Reed.

Q. Who are the three race officials who have worked on every Boilermaker?

A. Earle Reed, David Reichert and Dick Mattia.

Q. What radio station broadcasts the race, start to finish, every year?

A. WIBX.

Q. In terms of media coverage, what happened for the first time at the 1993 race?

A. WKTV and WUTR provided live television coverage.

Q. How many volunteers work on the race?

A. More than 1,000.

Q. How long is the Boilermaker?

A. 9.3 miles.

Q. Who won the first Boilermaker?

A. The 1978 winners were Ric Rojas of Colorado, who finished in 45 minutes, 38 seconds, and Kathy Mills of Syracuse, 54 minutes, 26 seconds.

Q. The number of runners in the Boilermaker has increased every year except which one?

A. 1986.

Q. How many people attend the Boilermaker Health & Fitness Expo, the day before the race?

A. An estimated 15,000 to 20,000.

Q. How many booths are there at the Expo?

A. 65.

Q. How many youngsters participate in the Boilermaker Youth Run?

A. 800.

Q. How many aid stations are on the Boilermaker course?

A. 14.

Q. How many water cups do those aid stations use?

A. A total of 65,000.

Q. How many orange slices were handed out at the 1993 race?

A. 11,000.

Q. How many sponges were handed out at the 1993 race?

A. 7,000.

Q. What was the amount of ice used during the 1993 race?

A. 750 bags, each containing eight pounds of ice.

Q. How much Boilermaker prize money is awarded each year?

A. $35,000.

Q. What is the bonus given to the male or female runner setting a course record?

A. $1,000.

Q. Where does the race start?

A. Utica Boilers, east Utica.

Q. Where does the race end?

A. F.X. Matt Brewing Company, west Utica.

THE SPORTING LIFE

CHAPTER SIX

Q. Who is Donovan Field, home of the Blue Sox, named after?

A. The late State Senator James Donovan, who secured state funding to improve the field.

Q. How high is the stadium's center field fence?

A. 12 feet.

Q. How many lights for night games are there at Donovan?

A. 76.

Q. How wide is the outfield warning track?

A. 15 feet.

Q. What material was used to make the infield?

A. Red clay.

Q. What are the distances to the outfield fences?

A. 324 feet to right and left, and 390 feet to center field.

Q. Donovan Stadium is in what field?

A. Murnane Field, named after Charles Murnane, a young baseball and football coach in the Utica School District who died in 1939.

Q. Murnane Field is in what park?

A. Horatio Seymour Park, named in honor of a former Utica mayor and New York governor.

Q. Why is America's Greatest Heart Run & Walk, held every February in Utica, so named?

A. It raises more money than any other American Heart Association run-walk of its kind in the country.

Q. Who is known as Mister Heart Run?

A. Jim Simpson, chairman of America's Greatest Heart Run & Walk.

Q. How many lanes are at the Pin-O-Rama bowling alley?

A. 48.

Q. What village was once known as "the biggest little hockey town in the United States"?

A. Clinton, N.Y., home of the Comets.

Q. What was the name of the local semi-pro football team of the 1960s and '70s?

A. The Utica-Rome Chiefs.

Q. What positions did Ted McQuade and Wayne Robinson play for the Chiefs?

A. Quarterback and safety.

Q. Al (Bobey) Salerno worked in what sport?

A. He was a major league baseball umpire, 1961-1968.

Q. In what sport did Val Bialas excel?

A. He was a member of the U.S. Olympic speed skating team in 1924, 1928, and 1932.

Q. At what other sport did Bialas excel?

A. He was Utica's public tennis court champion five times.

Q. What put an end to Bialas' competitive skating?

A. Because of a car accident in 1935, his right leg had to be amputated.

Q. Did he ever skate or play tennis again?

A. Yes, he gave skating exhibitions and instructions and won several tennis tournaments playing doubles.

Q. What position in Utica city government did Bialas later assume?

A. In 1962, Mayor Frank Dulan appointed Bialas as parks commissioner.

Q. What Utica recreation area was named in honor of Val Bialas?

A. The Val Bialas Ski Center on the Parkway.

Q. How many chairs are there on the chairlift at the Val Bialas Ski Center?

A. The lift is 1,800 feet long and has 71 chairs.

Q. Proctor High School's Dave Cash played major league baseball for what teams?

A. Cash, a 1966 Proctor graduate, played for the Pittsburgh Pirates, Philadelphia Phillies, Montreal Expos and San Diego Padres.

Q. What two area natives are now playing baseball in the major leagues?

A. Mark Lemke and Andy Van Slyke.

Q. Where did Atlanta Braves second baseman Mark Lemke attend high school?

A. Notre Dame High School, Burrstone Road.

Q. Where in the draft was Lemke selected?

A. Atlanta picked him in the 27th round of the 1983 draft.

Q. When was Lemke's major league debut?

A. Sept. 17, 1988.

Q. When was Lemke's first major league hit?

A. Sept. 18, 1988, a single off San Diego's Andy Hawkins.

Q. Where did Pittsburgh Pirate center fielder Andy Van Slyke attend high school?

A. New Hartford.

Q. Where in the draft was Van Slyke selected?

A. He was the number one pick of the St. Louis Cardinals in the 1979 draft.

Q. When was Van Slyke's major league debut?

A. June 17, 1983.

Q. When was Van Slyke's first major league hit?

A. A double off Chicago's Chuck Rainey, June 17, 1983.

Q. What unusual event occurred in the 1991 National League Championship Series to put the Utica area on the baseball map?

A. Lemke and Van Slyke played against each other.

Q. Besides being major league baseball players, what do Mark Lemke, Andy Van Slyke, George Wiltse of Hamilton, George Burns of Utica, Hal Schumacher of Dolgeville, Karl Spooner of Oriskany Falls and Dave Cash have in common?

A. At one time or another, all of them played in the World Series.

Q. What position did Proctor High School's Ted Lepcio play in the major leagues?

A. Lepcio was an infielder with the Boston Red Sox, 1952-58; the Detroit Tigers, 1959-60, and the Philadelphia Phillies, Chicago White Sox and Minnesota Twins, 1961-62.

Q. What rare thing happened in Lepcio's first game as a Detroit Tiger?

A. He hit a grand slam home run and beat his old team, the Red Sox.

Q. How many years has New Hartford's Wayne Levi been on the PGA Tour?

A. As of 1993, it has been 17 years.

Q. How much money has Levi won playing golf on the tour?

A. As of 1993, nearly $4 million.

Q. Why was 1990 such a good year for Levi?

A. He won four tournaments, earned more than $1 million and was named PGA Tour Player of the Year.

Q. When was the Utica Curling Club established?

A. In 1868.

Q. What Utican once held the world's indoor record for the high jump?

A. Irving K. Baxter, who attended Utica Free Academy in the 1890s, set the record by jumping 6 feet, 3.5 inches, and he won gold medals in high jump and pole vault at the Olympics in Paris, 1900.

Q. What brought legendary Notre Dame football coach Knute Rockne to Utica?

A. His team was taking the train back to college after a game in New York City and Rockne used a short layover in Utica to march his players from Union Station to St. John's Church for Mass.

Q. What were Heintz, Roger's, Rainbow, Empire, Palace, and Royal?

A. Bowling alleys.

Q. What Utica company at one time had the largest line of fishing tackle in the world?

A. Horrocks-Ibbotson, on Whitesboro Street near Genesee.

Q. Before television, what did the Observer-Dispatch put on the roof of its building during the World Series?

A. A large scoreboard to announce the inning-by-inning score of the game.

Q. In what sport did Whitesboro's Joe Ficcaro excel?

A. Marathon running.

Q. What New Hartford runner has set national age group records?

A. Howard Rubin.

Q. Where did the Utica Blue Sox of the old Class A Eastern League play home games?

A. McConnell Field in north Utica, about where the Red Roof Inn is now located.

Q. What was McConnell Field's nickname?

A. Because of its wooden seats, it was known as Splinter Haven.

Q. What are the colors of the Utica Bulldogs hockey team?

A. Orange, black and white with a bulldog logo.

Q. Who is the Bulldog's owner?

A. Skip Probst.

Q. What was "Star of the West"?

A. A Utica cricket club of the mid-1800s.

Q. Where in Utica was cricket played?

A. Near City Hall, about where the Kennedy Towers apartments now stand.

Q. Professional baseball in Utica began when?

A. The Utica Baseball Club was formed in 1878.

Q. Where did the Utica Baseball Club play its home games?

A. At a baseball field near today's Harbor Point Inn on north Genesee Street.

Q. What is the second oldest high school cross country race in New York State?

A. The E.J. Herrmann Invitational, now in its 51st year, is run in Proctor Park.

Q. Who was E.J. Herrmann?

A. The late E.J. Herrmann was a high school running coach for more than 50 years in the Utica school district.

Q. What distinction once belonged to Herrmann?

A. He was the oldest cross country coach in the United States.

CHEERS FOR GREAT MATT'S BEERS

CHAPTER SEVEN

Q. How many light bulbs are in the Utica Club sign atop the F.X. Matt Brewing Company's brewery in west Utica?

A. 1,950.

Q. Where was F.X. Matt I, founder of the brewery, born?

A. The Black Forest region of west Germany in 1859.

Q. At what age did Matt retire?

A. He was active in the business until he died at age 99.

Q. Before its name was changed to the F.X. Matt Brewing Company, what was the company called?

A. The West End Brewing Company.

Q. When was the West End Brewing Company formed?

A. 1888.

Q. Why was it named West End?

A. Because of its location in the west end of Utica.

Q. The West End Brewing Company is a direct outgrowth of what other brewery?

A. Carl Bierbauer's Columbia Brewery, which was reorganized into the West End Brewery by Matt when Bierbauer died.

Q. How many employees worked at West End in its first year?

A. 12.

Q. What Matt's products were made during Prohibition?

A. Soft drink, fruit beverages, malt syrup, malt tonic and "near beer," which contained no alcohol.

Q. What impressive feat did the brewery achieve at the end of Prohibition in 1933?

A. Matt's was the first brewery in the United States to obtain a permit to sell beer - 90 minutes after Prohibition's repeal.

Q. What happened at the brewery on the first night beer was made legal?

A. Thousands of people formed lines in front of the brewery waiting to buy the first bottles available.

Q. How many people have taken the F.X. Matt Brewery Tour?

A. Visitor number 2,000,000 took the tour on Aug. 18, 1993.

Q. When did the brewery's Tour Center open its doors to the public?

A. Feb. 15, 1965.

Q. People from how many states have signed the guest book?

A. Every state.

Q. Representatives from how many countries have taken the tour?

A. More than 100, ranging from Afghanistan to Yugoslavia.

Q. How long does a brewery tour take?

A. About 90 minutes.

Q. What do doctors Nestor Herbowy, Tom Webb, Tom LaFountain; attorneys Gerald Popeo, Stewart Roberts, Larry George; insurance company owner Larry Gilroy; and photographer Guy Danella have in common?

A. All were former brewery tour guides.

Q. Who was the brewery's first female tour guide?

A. Mary Therese (T.C.) Callahan, now of the Uptown Grill.

Q. Who was the long-time Tour Center hostess?

A. Carolyn Kapolka greeted brewery visitors for 28 years.

Q. Was Kapolka the Tour Center's first hostess?

A. Vivian Stevenson and Rosemary Dinger had the job for a few months before Kapolka.

Q. Who succeeded Kapolka as Tour Center hostess?

A. Tricia Heston took over the job in May, 1993.

Q. What is the name of the tavern where the brewery tour ends?

A. The 1888 Tavern.

Q. What is the name's significance?

A. It was the year the brewery was founded.

Q. Before it was converted into a two-floor tour center in 1965, how was the building used?

A. As a warehouse, and before that it was used for bottling.

Q. Is anything besides samples of Matt's beer served in the tavern?

A. Draft root beer.

Q. What is the root beer's name?

A. The root beer is a blend made especially for the brewery by Pepsi, and has no name.

Q. What size beer mugs are used in the tavern?

A. 12 ounce.

Q. In what movie does a bottle of Utica Club beer show up in a couple of scenes?

A. "Dirty Dancing."

Q. What best-selling author makes reference to Matt's beer in his books?

A. Stephen King.

Q. What other popular author has a habit of mentioning Matt's products in his books?

A. Mystery writer Robert B. Parker.

Q. When Matt's started brewing beer in Utica in 1888, how many breweries were there in the city?

A. Twelve, and Matt's (West End) was the smallest.

Q. What nationally famous athletic event is tied to the brewery?

A. The Boilermaker Road Race finishes at the brewery's front door.

Q. When F.X. Matt died, who took over as company president?

A. His son, Walter.

Q. Who took over from Walter Matt?

A. His son, F.X. Matt II.

Q. Who took over as company president from F.X. Matt II?

A. His younger brother, Nicholas Matt.

Q. What does F.X. Matt II, now chairman of the board, do every working day?

A. Upholding a tradition started by his grandfather and continued by his father, F.X. tours the brewery.

Q. What did F.X. Matt II once do to promote his beers?

A. Beginning in 1981, he starred in a series of television commericals.

Q. What does F.X. stand for?

A. Francis Xavier.

Q. What are the names of the talking beer steins who served as "spokesmugs" for the Utica Club line of beers?

A. Schultz and Dooley.

Q. What happened when the brewery introduced Schultz and Dooley?

A. Sales increased more than 50 percent.

Q. Schultz and Dooley had what kind of accents?

A. Schultz had a gruff voice and a German accent. Dooley had a sweet voice and an Irish brogue.

Q. What famous comedian was the voice for Schultz and Dooley?

A. Jonathan Winters.

Q. Who was the puppeteer who brought Schultz and Dooley to life?

A. The late Bil Baird of New York City.

Q. What are the names of the other talking beer steins in the Utica Club?

A. The Countess, Bubbles LaBrew, Officer Sudds, U-Cee, Farmer Mugee, Cousin Emma, Fireman Fritz and Old Man Stein.

Q. Where are the mugs sold?

A. The Brewery Shop, next door to the brewery's Tour Center in a building that once was the Rainbow Grill.

Q. When did the Brewery Shop open?

A. 1981.

Q. What innovative packaging did the brewery pioneer?

A. The plastic Beerball container.

Q. How much beer is in a Beerball?

A. 5.17 gallons.

Q. When did Matt's start putting beer in cans?

A. 1935.

Q. Why is the brewery's Maximus Super such a distinctive beer?

A. With an alcohol content of 6.5 percent, it is one of the most potent beers in the country.

Q. What limited edition beer does the brewery make every Thanksgiving and Christmas?

A. Season's Best Holiday Amber.

Q. What is unique about the brewery's Freeport USA drink?

A. It is the only alcohol-free brew in the country.

Q. What slogan, which was never used in advertising, was used by Walter Matt to describe Matt's Premium?

A. "Unique in its excellence."

Q. What form of writing does F.X. Matt II enjoy?

A. He composes limericks.

Q. What is the first job F.X. Matt II had at the brewery?

A. Starting in 1949, while in college, he worked summers in the bottling plant, loaded trucks and delivered beer kegs to bars.

KEWPEE'S: HAMBURGER HEAVEN

CHAPTER EIGHT

Q. What is Kewpee's slogan?

A. "Hamburg pickle on top makes your heart go flippity-flop."

Q. Where was Kewpee's?

A. On Genesee Street at Oneida Square, now the site of Burger King.

Q. When was Kewpee's torn down?

A. The winter of 1973.

Q. How many Kewpee's remain in the United States?

A. Six.

Q. Where are those remaining Kewpee's?

A. Three are in Lima, Ohio; two in Lansing, Mich., and one in Racine, Wis.

Q. Who owns the Kewpee's trademark?

A. Harry Shutt, who owns the three Kewpee's in Lima, Ohio.

Q. What color are the Kewpee's hamburger wrappers?

A. Blue and white.

Q. What famous hamburger entrepreneur said he "learned a lot" from Kewpee's?

A. Dave Thomas, founder of Wendy's.

Q. What two forms of service were offered to Kewpee's customers?

A. Self service inside the restaurant and carhop service in the parking lot.

Q. What message was on the neon sign facing Kewpee's parking lot?

A. "Please do not blow horn. Use lights for service."

Q. What did ordering a hamburger "with everything" get you?

A. Ketchup, mustard, onion and pickle.

Q. What drink was famous at Kewpee's?

A. Frosted malts.

Q. Kewpee's was a hangout for what schools?

A. Utica College, which had its campus on Oneida Square in the 1950s, and nearby Utica Free Academy.

Q. What Kewpee's logo was above the front door?

A. A revolving Kewpee doll, which was illuminated at night.

Q. What were Kewpee's hours?

A. It never closed.

Q. What was done to Kewpee's hamburger rolls?

A. They were toasted.

Q. In what year was the Kewpee's chain of restaurants formed?

A. 1938.

Q. How many restaurants were in the Kewpee's chain?

A. At one point, there were 250, centered in the Midwest.

Q. When Kewpee's opened in Utica, the hamburgers sold for how much?

A. 10 cents.

Q. Each booth at Kewpee's came equipped with what?

A. A small jukebox attached to the wall, a few inches above the table, three songs for a quarter.

Q. What was said to be the secret behind the great taste of Kewpee's hamburgers?

A. The beef was ground fresh daily.

EAT, DRINK AND BE MERRY

CHAPTER NINE

Q. What long-time bartender at the Uptown Grill was the father of a Utica councilman?

A. The late Howard Welch tended bar at the Uptown and his son, Howard, is majority leader of the Common Council.

Q. What is on the roof at Voss's hot dog stand in Yorkville?

A. A giant milk bottle.

Q. What famous hot dog and hamburger place on Seneca Turnpike was named after a meal?

A. The Chili Hut.

Q. Where was Sal's Barbecue?

A. The drive-in was on Oriskany Boulevard, Yorkville, now the site of Holland Farms Dairy.

Q. What south Utica restaurant, famous for its fish fry, once prohibited unescorted women from standing at the bar?

A. The Uptown Grill.

Q. Where were Utica's two White Tower restaurants located?

A. The 24-hour hamburger joints were both on Genesee Street, one near Oriskany Street and the other in south Utica.

Q. What unique service did Donalty's and Callahan's, a saloon that was once on Broad and John streets, provide?

A. Since women were not permitted in the bar, take-out service was allowed and couples sat outside and drank beer in their cars.

Q. What two Blandina Street bars were torn down to make room for the New York State Office Building?

A. Roach & Quinn and The Kirk.

Q. Jean's Beans, on Hampden Place behind the Uptown Theater, was famous for what Friday night meal?

A. Fish fry.

Q. Where was King Cole Ice Cream located?

A. In the shopping center now occupied by Marine Midland Bank, Genesee at Arnold Avenue.

Q. Where was Club Stanek?

A. At 1714 Burrstone Road, in a building now occupied by St. Luke's-Memorial Hospital's Dental Services.

Q. Before it was Pensero's Restaurant, what was it?

A. Mayo Gate, a popular Irish bar operated by one John Oakes, and before that it was Lange's Restaurant.

Q. Where was The Lamp Lighter Room?

A. The bar was in the old Hotel Utica.

Q. What were two brands of beer produced at the Eagle Brewing Company?

A. Peerless Lager and Monarch Ale.

Q. The building next to Friendly Ice Cream on Genesee Street is now home to the China Garden Restaurant, but what used to be there?

A. The Green Lantern Restaurant, and before that it was an eating establishment called Otto and Karl's.

Q. On what street were these restaurants and nightspots: Elgin Diner, Silver Rail, Lincoln Farms, Sheridan's, Brassel's and the Waldorf Cafeteria?

A. Lafayette Street, between Genesee and Washington.

Q. What were Oneida, Fort Schuyler, Gulf, Utica and Starr?

A. Utica breweries.

Q. What were the Brown Jug, Old Shanty, Piccadilly, Checkerboard, Ten Pin, Charlie Parker's, Log Cabin and Chippewa?

A. All were once busy saloons and all are now out of business.

Q. What is the Oneida County Suncoast Picnic?

A. An annual gathering of past and present residents of Oneida County, who either winter in Florida or live there year round.

Q. Before it became Casa Too Mucha, what was the name of the bar occupying that site?

A. The Leather Bottle.

Q. What bar once occupied what is now a parking lot on the east side of the Observer-Dispatch?

A. In the 1960s, the Barbershop was a popular drinking spot for young people.

Q. Tiny's Grill on State Street was originally called what?

A. The Oneida Grill.

Q. Before it became The Columbia, the bar at Columbia and State streets had what name?

A. The Blue Label Grill.

Q. What famous eating place was once in the small shopping plaza at the point of Route 8 and Route 12 in north Utica?

A. Northern Lights, a hot dog stand.

THE NEWS MEDIA

| CHAPTER TEN |

Q. What former WKTV newscaster is married to New York City politician Rudolph Giuliani?

A. Donna Hanover.

Q. What long time "farm radio" personality has been a member of the New York State Fair Advisory Board since 1954?

A. Ed Slusarczyk.

Q. What double distinction did Donna Donovan achieve at the Observer-Dispatch?

A. She was the first female executive editor and the first female publisher.

Q. How old is the Observer-Dispatch?

A. The Observer was merged with the Herald-Dispatch in 1922 to form the Observer-Dispatch.

Q. What was Utica's first radio station?

A. Technically, that distinction goes to a station operated by J & M Electric Company, Bank Place, which operated in 1922 at low power and broadcasted only periodically.

Q. What was Utica's first regularly scheduled radio station?

A. WIBX, which obtained its license in 1925.

Q. Where did WIBX once have its offices and studio?

A. In 1926, the station moved into rooms at the Hotel Utica.

Q. What was the Saturday Globe?

A. A weekly newspaper, which started publishing in Utica in 1881.

Q. Who subscribed to the Globe?

A. England's Queen Victoria, President Grover Cleveland, and 294,000 others in this country and around the world.

Q. What made the Globe so special?

A. It pioneered the use of illustrations, cartoons, and color.

Q. How did Globe editors localize the newspaper for various parts of the country?

A. By having 50 editions.

Q. How successful was the Globe's circulation system?

A. So successful that Saturday Evening Post officials came to Utica to study the Globe's plan.

Q. Whose picture was the first to appear in the Globe?

A. Horatio Seymour, a Utica mayor and New York governor.

Q. Where was the Globe's office and plant?

A. North side of Whitesboro Street, a few doors west of Genesee.

Q. How powerful was the Globe?

A. Albert Dickinson, Globe managing editor, once got the execution of a condemned man advanced so it would meet the newspaper's deadline.

Q. What line of work did Albert Dickinson's daughter, Alberta, go into?

A. Alberta was a talented reporter and worked for many years at the Observer-Dispatch.

Q. When did WUTR-TV first go on the air?

A. March, 1970.

Q. What former WUTR anchor is now an attorney?

A. Fran Cafarell.

Q. What former Utica newspaper reporter wrote "Murder in the Adirondacks"?

A. Craig Brandon.

Q. Who was Harold Frederic and what newspaper distinction did he achieve in 1880?

A. Frederic, who also wrote novels, became editor of the Utica Observer at the young age 24.

Q. What was Frederic's most famous book?

A. "The Damnation of Theron Ware."

Q. Where was Frederic born?

A. On South Street, 1856.

Q. What other newspapers did Frederic work for?

A. He was editor of the Albany Journal and European correspondent for The New York Times.

Q. What did Jerry Fiore, Joe Roser, Lyle Bosley and Bob Lewis have in common?

A. All were broadcasters on WKTV.

Q. Who was Dante Tranquille?

A. Chief photographer for the Observer-Dispatch and The Utica Daily Press.

Q. What WIBX announcer was known as the "voice of the Clinton Comets"?

A. The late Ralph Allinger.

Q. What did Len Wilbur, Phil Spartano and Bill Higdon have in common?

A. All were long-time sports editors of the Observer-Dispatch and The Utica Daily Press.

Q. Who was the host of WKTV's weekly Outdoor Sportsmen Show?

A. Jack Fredericks.

Q. When did WKTV first go on the air?

A. Thursday, Dec. 1, 1949.

Q. How many television stations were there in the United States on Dec. 1, 1949?

A. Fewer than 100.

Q. In those early days, what hours was WKTV on the air?

A. The station signed on at 5:30 p.m. and signed off at 11 p.m.

Q. What was the first program broadcast by WKTV?

A. Kukla, Fran and Ollie.

Q. What WKTV announcer played Bozo the Clown?

A. Ed Whittaker.

Q. What former Observer-Dispatch government reporter is now an assistant attorney general in Pennsylvania?

A. Tim Rice.

Q. What one thing do Gilbert Smith, Mason Taylor, Donna Donovan and Jack Marsh have in common?

A. All are former executive editors of the Observer-Dispatch.

Q. Who was David Beetle?

A. An award-winning Utica newspaper reporter who wrote "Along the Oriskany," "Up Old Forge Way" and "West Canada Creek."

Q. In what year did the Observer-Dispatch and The Utica Daily Press win a Pulitzer Gold Medal for meritorious public service?

A. 1959.

Q. What did the newspapers do to win journalism's highest award?

A. Reported on graft and corruption in city government.

Q. What two reporters did the bulk of the reporting that resulted in that Pulitzer Prize?

A. Anthony Vella, who went on to become managing editor of the Observer-Dispatch, and William Lohden, who became editorial writer of the The Utica Daily Press, worked under the direction of Mason Taylor, executive editor.

Q. What former editorial writer for the Observer-Dispatch is now a diplomat with the U.S. State Department?

A. George Newman.

Q. What statue is on the Memorial Parkway at the intersection of Holland Avenue?

A. A memorial to George Dunham (1859-1922), editor of The Utica Daily Press and one of the city's most public-spirited citizens.

Q. What famous downtown business once owned radio station WIBX?

A. The Boston Store owned the station for a short time in 1928.

Q. What did Dick Costa do at the Observer-Dispatch?

A. He wrote a column called "The Costa Living."

Q. For many years Frank Tomaino, city editor of the Observer-Dispatch, wrote a column called?

A. "FRANKly Speaking."

Q. What was the name of the long-time column written by Observer-Dispatch editor Harold Whittemore?

A. "It's the Little Things."

Q. What was the first newspaper in New York State west of Albany?

A. The Whitestown Gazette, this area's first newspaper.

Q. When did the Whitestown Gazette start publishing?

A. July 10, 1793, in New Hartford, which was then part of Whitestown.

Q. When did the Observer-Dispatch become a member of the Gannett group of newspapers?

A. In 1922, a group headed by Frank Gannett bought the Utica Sunday Tribune, the Herald-Dispatch, the Utica Observer and joined the papers under the name Utica Observer-Dispatch.

BUSINESS - BIG, SMALL AND IN BETWEEN

CHAPTER ELEVEN

Q. What ex-Utican struck it rich in Las Vegas?

A. Steve Wynn, chairman of the board, Golden Nugget Inc., which owns the Mirage casino and hotel, among other things.

Q. What are Wynn's connections to Utica?

A. He attended Kemble and John F. Hughes elementary schools, and his father operated a bingo parlor here.

Q. Where in Utica did the Wynns live?

A. On the Parkway near Genesee Street and at 2230 Douglas Crescent.

Q. Were there any other area connections?

A. For many years Steve Wynn and his family vacationed in the Old Forge area.

Q. What does the sign on the west wall of the Doyle Hardware Store, Broad and First streets, state?

A. It announces that the store was established in 1872.

Q. What are the names of the cows on the billboard outside Holland Farms, Oriskany Street, Yorkville?

A. Cupcake and Chuckie.

Q. How were the names chosen?

A. Suggestions were submitted by customers.

Q. During the 1950s, where in Utica did Irene Burke conduct "business"?

A. Her brothel was on Pearl Street, a stone's throw from the old City Hall.

Q. When did Riverside Mall open?

A. 1974.

Q. What were Riverside Mall's original three anchor stores?

A. J.M. Fields, Howlands and Montgomery Ward.

Q. What downtown intersection once got so much traffic it was called the Busy Corner?

A. The intersection of Genesee, Bleecker and Lafayette.

Q. What drug store chain had a store on the northeast corner of the Busy Corner for many years?

A. Daw Drug.

Q. Daw Drug, which had stores throughout the Utica area, was taken over by what chain?

A. Rite Aid Pharmacies.

Q. Who was affectionately known as the "mayor of downtown"?

A. Syd Oberman, owner of Oberman's Clothes, on the Busy Corner.

Q. What special service did Hathaway Bakery provide to its customers?

A. It delivered bakery goods right to their door.

Q. Who was Henry Kaiser?

A. Kaiser got his start in Utica and went on to form the Kaiser Jeep Corporation, and his construction company built Boulder Dam, Grand Coulee Dam, and the San Francisco-Oakland Bay Bridge.

Q. Who was Charles Mott?

A. He started building wheels in Utica when the automotive industry was just beginning, and his Utica company later became part of General Motors.

Q. What ill-fated model of car was once sold on South Street between Seymour and Howard?

A. Edsel.

Q. What prevented Utica banks from failing in the early 1930s?

A. Mrs. Thomas Proctor used her fortune to keep the banks afloat.

Q. What was the Square-Vue?

A. An Oneida Square luncheonette, which catered to generations of Utica Free Academy students.

Q. What was Chuck's?

A. Another gathering place for UFA students, corner of Elm and Gold streets.

Q. What boast was once made by the now-defunct Mohawk Valley Cap Company?

A. It claimed to be the biggest cap factory in the United States.

Q. What was the Rope Walk?

A. Located in a long building that ran east and west between Kemble and Oneida streets, rope was manufactured there, including the rope which hanged Charles Guiteau, assassin of President Garfield.

Q. What brand of cigarettes was once manufactured in a factory on West Street?

A. Cardinals.

Q. What downtown Utica bakery had this slogan on its delivery trucks: "Hit me easy, I'm full of pie"?

A. The Red Cherry Pie Shop, Charlotte Street, across from the Oneida County Office Building.

Q. Where was Chanatry's first grocery store?

A. In 1912, three Chanatry brothers, Michael, Raymond and Yorhaky, opened for business in the 500 block of Bleecker Street, selling produce and Syrian pita bread baked by their wives.

Q. What was England & McCaffrey?

A. A landmark drug store on Genesee Street, near Columbia, which featured a marble-topped soda fountain.

Q. Where in Utica were organs and pianos once made?

A. The Buhl Organ Company was on the east side of Seymour Avenue, between South and Rutger, until it went out of business in the 1960s.

Q. During the busy shopping days leading up to Christmas, what public service was performed in downtown Utica by Boy Scouts in the 1950s and 1960s?

A. Using poles, tipped with red flags, they held back pedestrians until the traffic light turned green.

Q. What does the PAR in PAR Technology Corporation stand for?

A. Pattern Analysis and Recognition.

Q. Where in downtown Utica did Helen Hoffman once sell newspapers and magazines without paying rent?

A. She set up a squatter's shack on the sidewalk next to the south wall of the Marine Midland Bank on Columbia Street near Genesee.

Q. What was the name of the magazine once published by the Savings Bank of Utica and given to its customers?

A. "The Way To Wealth," a magazine filled with information about the bank and the area, was published in the 1930s and '40s.

Q. Who founded the Savings Bank of Utica?

A. Brothers John and Nicholas Devereux.

Q. How did the bank get started?

A. The Devereux brothers operated a general store at Bagg's Square in 1814 and Uticans, who respected their honesty, gave cash to them for safe keeping.

Q. When did the Devereux brothers apply for a charter to formally establish a bank?

A. 1821.

Q. Who was the Savings Bank of Utica's first president?

A. John Devereux.

Q. What sites has the Savings Bank of Utica occupied over the years?

A. Bagg's Square, Bleecker Street, the southwest corner of Genesee and Lafayette streets, and since 1900 on the northeast corner of Genesee and Bank Place.

Q. How big is the Utica Business Park?

A. 82 acres.

Q. What was once on the business park site?

A. The Utica College Golf Course.

Q. What was there before the golf course?

A. Rhoads Hospital, a World War II military hospital.

Q. What was there before Rhoads Hospital?

A. A farm.

Q. The Home Telephone Company started in Utica in 1903 and their operators provided what services?

A. Information on telephone numbers, weather forecasts, baseball scores and wake-up calls.

Q. Who was Merwin K. Hart and what did he start in 1914?

A. The Utica Mutual Compensation Insurance Corporation, forerunner of today's Utica National Insurance Group.

Q. What distinction did Ethel Weiss, who later became Mrs. Ethel Wood, achieve at Utica Mutual?

A. On Feb. 12, 1914, she became the company's first employee and she didn't retire until 51 years later.

Q. What once occupied the site on which the Utica National Insurance Group has its headquarters in New Hartford?

A. The Country Day School, and before that several holes of the Yahnundasis Golf Club were located about where the insurance company's buildings stand today.

Q. When did construction start on the Utica National Insurance Group's building?

A. Ground was broken in December, 1950, but the Korean War caused a shortage of building materials and the cornerstone wasn't laid until May 10, 1952.

Q. What was in the sealed copper box that was placed in the cornerstone?

A. Forty-eight items, including Utica Mutual's original charter, minutes from the company's first annual meeting, and the first policy issued; copies of the Observer-Dispatch, The Utica Daily Press, and New York Times; a 1914 penny and 1952 half-dollar.

Q. Before moving to New Hartford, where were Utica Mutual's offices located?

A. The company occupied the top six floors of the First National Bank Building (now the Bankers Trust Building), northeast corner of Genesee and Elizabeth.

Q. Utica Mutual adopted what slogan in 1964?

A. "Insurance That Starts With You."

Q. Where in Utica was a match factory once located?

A. In the 1800s, Eaton & Son had a factory at Conkling Avenue and South Street.

Q. What eventually happened to the match factory?

A. It became part of the Diamond Match Company in 1881 and made matches in Utica until 1883.

POLITICS and GOVERNMENT

CHAPTER TWELVE

Q. Look closely and what can be seen on the official seal of the City of Utica?

A. An Indian, wearing a headdress and carrying a quiver of arrows on his back, is standing in front of two teepees, and there are two log cabins on each side of the Indian, two pine trees behind the teepees, a tree behind one of the cabins, and an Indian paddling a boat.

Q. What color is the official City of Utica flag?

A. Gold with a multi-colored city seal in the center.

Q. How many proclamations did Mayor Louis LaPolla issue in 1992?

A. 251.

Q. How many people were married by Mayor LaPolla in 1992?

A. 130.

Q. Who was the highest ranking politician in area history?

A. James Schoolcraft Sherman, vice president of the United States, 1909-12, during the Taft administration.

Q. What ended Sherman's political career?

A. In 1912, he was nominated to run again with Taft, but Sherman died six days before Election Day at age 57.

Q. How many people attended Sherman's wake?

A. About 25,000 paid their respects, including President Taft.

Q. What was one of the jobs Frank Dulan had before being elected Utica's mayor in 1959?

A. He delivered ice.

Q. What mayor served in both the old City Hall and the new City Hall?

A. Frank Dulan.

Q. Who was Utica's mayor during its sesquicentennial celebration?

A. Stephen Pawlinga was mayor when the city celebrated its 150th birthday in 1982.

Q. Who was president of the Utica Common Council when Stephen Pawlinga was mayor?

A. Edward Rewkowski.

Q. What high-ranking judicial office was achieved by Ward Hunt?

A. Hunt, who was Utica's mayor in 1844, was appointed to the U.S. Supreme Court by President Grant in 1872.

Q. What Utica lawyer and politician turned down an appointment to become chief justice of the U.S. Supreme Court, offered by President Grant?

A. Roscoe Conkling, mayor of Utica in 1858, congressman, 1859-67, U.S. Senator, 1867-1881.

Q. What mayoral distinction is held by Fred J. Douglas, who was elected to that office in 1921?

A. Douglas, chief surgeon at Faxton Hospital, was the only doctor ever elected mayor of Utica.

Q. What Utica mayor is thought to have committed suicide?

A. Although one report claimed that Charles Doolittle was "swept overboard" on a trip to Europe in 1874, most newspapers advanced the belief that the man who had been elected mayor 21 years earlier actually jumped.

Q. What statue is on the west side of Genesee Street at the Memorial Parkway?

A. Utica's James Schoolcraft Sherman, vice president of the United States.

Q. Michael Caruso, mayor from 1972 through 1973, was in what kind of business before his election?

A. He owned a cheese company.

Q. Who was the only Utican ever elected governor of New York State?

A. Horatio Seymour.

Q. What was unique about Seymour's time as governor?

A. He was elected to the office twice, 1853-55, and 1863-65.

Q. Has a New York State attorney general ever come from Utica?

A. Four of them: Samuel Talcott, 1819; Greene Bronson, 1829; Samuel Beardsley, 1836; John Davies, 1898.

Q. What was printed on the sign Mayor Edward Hanna placed on the wall behind his desk at City Hall?

A. "This City Government Belongs To The People."

Q. Where in the area did President Grover Cleveland spend part of his boyhood?

A. Clinton.

Q. What president's parents are buried in Holland Patent?

A. The Rev. and Mrs. Richard Cleveland, parents of President Grover Cleveland.

Q. To what position did President William McKinley appoint Utica's Ellis Roberts?

A. Roberts, who had been editor of the Utica Morning Herald and a congressman, was appointed treasurer of the United States.

Q. Who are the only two Uticans ever elected to the U.S. Senate?

A. Roscoe Conkling and Francis Kernan.

Q. What was unique about this?

A. From 1875 until 1881, they were in the Senate at the same time.

Q. What was the occupation of Dominick Assaro, mayor of Utica from 1968 through 1971?

A. Funeral director.

Q. What was the ethnic significance of Mayor Assaro's election?

A. He was the city's first mayor of Italian origin.

Q. Who was the first person of Lebanese origin to be elected mayor of Utica?

A. Edward Hanna, 1974-77.

Q. Who was the first person of Polish extraction to be elected mayor of Utica?

A. Stephen Pawlinga, 1978-83.

Q. What happened in 1859 when John Hoyt, the Republican, and Charles Wilson, the Democrat, each got 1,739 votes in Utica's mayoral election?

A. The matter was decided by the Common Council, which elected Wilson.

Q. Why is the downtown branch of the Utica Post Office named Butterfield Station?

A. It's named in honor of Utica's John Butterfield, who founded the Overland Mail, which later became the American Express Company, with Butterfield as its first president.

Q. Who once appointed members of Utica's police and fire department?

A. In the late 1800s, the power to make those appointments was in the hands of the Common Council.

BUILDINGS AND OTHER STRUCTURES

CHAPTER THIRTEEN

Q. Is the "Gold Dome" on top of the Savings Bank of Utica really gold?

A. The dome is covered with 23-karat gold leaf.

Q. What is unique about the Gold Dome?

A. It actually has two domes, one inside the other about 16 feet apart at the top, held together by a network of steel. The inner dome is the one seen inside the bank by customers.

Q. Why doesn't snow build up on the Gold Dome in the winter?

A. A circle of large radiators near the top of the inner dome provides heat to melt excessive snow from the outer dome.

Q. What is the outside diameter of the bank's Gold Dome?

A. 52 feet.

Q. How many floor tiles are there in the hallways at Riverside Mall?

A. 116,026.

Q. What is the tallest building in Utica?

A. The 17-story New York State Office Building.

Q. The second tallest?

A. The 15-story Bankers Trust Building, Genesee and Elizabeth streets.

Q. Where was the Halfway Bridge?

A. It once spanned Oriskany Street, connecting Utica and Yorkville.

Q. How many steps are there from the bottom of the New York State Office Building to the top?

A. 379.

Q. How many windows are there in the New York State office building?

A. 1,323.

Q. How many seats are there in the Stanley Performing Arts Center?

A. 2,963.

Q. What is the Stanley Performing Art Center's style of architecture?

A. Mexican Baroque inside and European Baroque outside.

Q. When was the Stanley built and at what cost?

A. In 1927 for $1.5 million.

Q. Why is the balcony staircase at the Stanley of special interest?

A. It is an exact replica of the grand staircase on the *Titanic.*

Q. What are the measurements of the Stanley's stage?

A. 60 feet wide, 43 feet deep, and 31 feet high.

Q. How many seats are there in the auditorium at Munson-Williams-Proctor Institute's Museum of Art?

A. 271.

Q. What do Fountain Elms, Utica Psychiatric Center, Stanley Performing Arts Center, Roscoe Conkling's House at 3 Rutger Park, St. Joseph-St. Patrick Church, and Union Station have in common?

A. All are on the National Register of Historic Places.

Q. What did it cost to build the Utica Memorial Auditorium?

A. The $4.5 million building opened on March 13, 1960.

Q. To what group is the Memorial Auditorium dedicated?

A. Men and women who died in defense of the country.

Q. What is the seating capacity of the Utica Memorial Auditorium?

A. Depending on the event, seating varies from a minimum of 3,972 to a maximum of 6,000.

Q. How much exhibition space does the auditorium have?

A. 24,000 square feet.

Q. What is special about the auditorium's roof?

A. A dual cable suspension system, which was the first of its kind in the world.

Q. What unusual order was given when the Bagg's Hotel was torn down in 1932?

A. Maria Proctor, owner of the hotel, ordered that it be torn down without the use of machines, thus providing work for as many people as possible during the Depression.

Q. Why was the Bagg's Memorial Building at Main and Genesee streets built?

A. To house records and memorabilia from Bagg's Hotel, which once stood on the site.

Q. What did it cost Maria Proctor to build the Bagg's Memorial Building?

A. $10,000.

Q. What happened to the records and memorabilia that were supposed to be housed there?

A. They disappeared before the building was completed.

Q. How was the Bagg's Memorial used during World War II?

A. Military police, on patrol at Union Station, used it as their headquarters.

Q. When did the Hotel Utica at Seneca and Lafayette streets open and what did it cost?

A. March 11, 1912, and the price was $610,000.

Q. What was the size of the original Hotel Utica?

A. 10 stories and 300 rooms.

Q. How was it enlarged?

A. In 1926, four more stories were added, bringing the number of rooms to 350.

Q. Where did the clock in the Tower of Hope at the new City Hall come from?

A. From the clock tower in the old City Hall, built in 1853 and demolished in 1968.

Q. Where was the old City Hall?

A. On the site of today's Radisson Hotel, Genesee Street.

Q. What happened to the 4,006-pound bell in the old City Hall clock tower?

A. It was melted down during World War II as part of the drive to collect scrap metal for the war effort.

Q. How tall is the Tower of Hope?

A. 100 feet.

Q. What did it cost to build the Tower of Hope?

A. $129,000.

Q. When and for whom was the Tower of Hope dedicated?

A. To Bob Hope, January, 1976.

Q. Who got the tower built?

A. Edward Hanna, who was mayor at the time.

Q. What was the "Hump?"

A. A Genesee Street bridge that crossed the Erie Canal, which once flowed along what is now Oriskany Street.

Q. What two buildings, which still stand, once housed the Utica Post Office?

A. The Alexander Pirnie Federal Building, Broad Street between Genesee and John streets, and Mechanics Hall, the corner of Liberty (Oriskany) and Hotel streets.

Q. What municipal building was once located at the end of Lincoln Avenue, corner of Burrstone Road?

A. A public bathhouse.

Q. Where was the Hotel Majestic?

A. Lafayette Street, next to Hotel Utica's west wall.

Q. What is the Hotel Majestic site used for today?

A. The hotel was torn down in 1963 and since then the site has been used as a parking lot.

Q. How did the Mayro Building, corner of Genesee Street and Bank Place, get its name?

A. By combining parts of the names of its builders Arthur MAYnard and Julius ROthstein.

Q. Allen Stem and Alfred Fellheimer designed Utica's Union Station and what other great train station?

A. They helped design New York City's Grand Central Station.

Q. Where was General Hospital located?

A. Southwest corner of Mohawk and South streets, now a shopping center.

Q. What does the City Hall dedication plaque state?

A. "Dedicated February 18, 1967 to the principle that there shall be government of the people, by the people and for the people forever."

Q. When was the City Hall cornerstone laid?

A. 1965.

Q. What was placed in the cornerstone?

A. Copies of The Utica Daily Press and New York Times, tapes of music provided by area radio stations, a video tape provided by WKTV, copies of city laws, and statements from city officials.

Q. Where does Gilmore Village, a municipal housing project in south Utica, get its name?

A. Frederick Gilmore, elected Utica's mayor in 1909, and again in 1923 and 1925, also served as city assessor, treasurer, and county sheriff.

Q. Where were Utica's public toilets once located?

A. In a building on the north side of Elizabeth Street between Genesee and Charlotte streets.

Q. What was unusual about these municipal restrooms?

A. They were underground.

Q. Old Fort Schuyler consisted of what?

A. Two log buildings, stockades and earthworks.

Q. When was St. John's Roman Catholic Church, on the southwest corner of John and Bleecker streets, first used by parishioners?

A. Christmas Day, 1869.

Q. How many other church buildings did St. John's have on the John and Bleecker site?

A. Two, the first church was built in 1821, the second in 1836.

MILITARY MATTERS

CHAPTER FOURTEEN

Q. Who is Soldiers and Sailors Monument on Oneida Square dedicated to?

A. Those who fought to save the Union during the Civil War.

Q. Where in Utica was a World War II German prisoner-of-war camp?

A. On the north side of Seward Avenue near Divine Brothers.

Q. What Utican composed Taps?

A. General Daniel Butterfield wrote the famous bugle call during the Civil War.

Q. How else did General Butterfield distinguish himself in the war?

A. He won the Congressional Medal of Honor.

Q. What happened to General Butterfield after the Civil War?

A. He went on to become assistant secretary of the U.S. Treasury Department.

Q. What other Utican was awarded the Medal of Honor during the Civil War?

A. Charles Cleveland, who later became Utica police chief, was cited for his bravery at Antietam.

Q. What Utican played a significant role in the Civil War as an aid to General Ulysses S. Grant?

A. Captain Samuel Beckwith, Grant's telegraph operator and cryptographer, was known as "Grant's Shadow" because he was always at the general's side.

Q. During World War II, how many soldiers were treated at Rhoads Hospital, which occupied the site of today's Utica Business Park?

A. When the hospital closed on July 1, 1946, a total of 25,277 had been treated.

Q. What was the hospital used for after the war?

A. One month after the hospital closed, it was reopened as Mohawk College, a state school for veterans.

Q. What was the site used for when Mohawk College closed in 1948?

A. Part of the land was used for Utica College's Golf Course, part of it went for Notre Dame and New York Mills high schools, and part for the Elihu Root Army Reserve Center on Burrstone Road.

Q. What Utican had a high-ranking position in President Theodore Roosevelt's cabinet?

A. Victor H. Metcalf, secretary of the Navy.

Q. How did Utica Cutlery Company play a part in World War II?

A. It produced 2 million bayonets, and millions of other knives for the military.

Q. How did Utica Radiator Corporation, now Utica Boilers, make an important contribution in the effort to win World War II?

A. The company manufactured magnesium alloy castings of parts for B-29s, the airplanes that bombed Japan.

Q. Savage Arms Company, which was housed in what is now CharlesTown, produced what weapons used in World War II?

A. Savage manufactured 300,000 Browning .50-caliber aircraft machine guns and 1,250,000 Thompson sub-machine guns.

Q. What did Bossert's in west Utica make during World War II?

A. The company turned out 20,000,000 artillery shell cases, 14,000 tank axles, and 300,000 oxygen cylinders for bomber flight crews.

Q. What important war items did Divine Brothers produce for the Army?

A. Bomb-loading devices and fuses for artillery shells.

Q. Why is Griffiss Air Force Base so named?

A. To honor Lt. Col. Townsend Griffiss who was killed in World War II.

Q. During World War II, how many surgical dressings were made by Red Cross volunteers in Utica?

A. 2,136,119.

Q. How much money did Uticans donate to the American Red Cross during World War II?

A. $878,259.

Q. How many pints of blood did Uticans donate to the armed forces during World War II?

A. 7,725.

THE MIGHTY "O"

CHAPTER FIFTEEN

Q. Where did the USS Oriskany get her name?

A. She was named after the American Revolutionary War's Battle of Oriskany.

Q. What kind of ship was the Oriskany?

A. An 899-foot long aircraft carrier that weighed 45,000 tons when fully loaded.

Q. What was the Oriskany's height?

A. Her flight deck was five stories above the water.

Q. What was the size of her crew?

A. She was equipped to handle a crew of 3,200.

Q. How many aircraft did she carry?

A. 80.

Q. What was her top speed?

A. 33 knots.

Q. How long did it take to build her?

A. 17 million working hours.

Q. Who paid for the Oriskany?

A. Area residents participated in four War Bond drives to raise $70 million to build her.

Q. What First Lady came to Utica to promote the sale of War Bonds to build the Oriskany?

A. Eleanor Roosevelt gave a stirring speech at Proctor High School.

Q. What did Mohawk Valley children do for the Oriskany's sailors?

A. They raised $2,000 to buy a piano and recreational equipment for the crew.

Q. What did Oriskany's crew do for Mohawk Valley children?

A. In the 1950s, when polio was crippling area children, the crew contributed $6,000 to the Oneida County Chapter of the National Foundation for Infantile Paralysis.

Q. When was the Oriskany launched?

A. Oct. 13, 1945 at the Brooklyn Navy Yard.

Q. How many people attended the launching ceremony?

A. 50,000.

Q. When was she commissioned?

A. September, 1950.

Q. What affiliation does John Iarrobino have with the Oriskany?

A. He was her captain during the Vietnam War.

Q. What is the Oriskany's nickname?

A. Mighty O.

Q. Where did the Oriskany serve in combat?

A. Korea and Vietnam.

Q. How did the Oriskany make history during the Korean War?

A. Aircraft from the Oriskany took part in the first multi-jet aerial dogfight in naval history, shooting down three Soviet MIG-15 jets.

Q. What well-known city did Oriskany flight crews bomb during the Vietnam war?

A. Hanoi.

Q. How else did the Oriskany make history?

A. She was the first aircraft carrier to sail around Cape Horn.

Q. What was the name of the ship's newspaper?

A. The Patriot, in honor of the patriots who fought at the Revolutionary War's Battle of Oriskany.

Q. What tragedy hit the Oriskany during the Vietnam War?

A. Fire broke out on the ship on Oct. 26, 1966, in the Gulf of Tonkin, killing 43 men, including Ensign Daniel Kern of Whitesboro.

Q. How did heroic sailors save the Oriskany from sinking during that fire?

A. By standing their ground against the fire and tossing 300 bombs, which were in reach of the flames, into the sea before they exploded.

Q. What was the Oriskany's connection to Hollywood?

A. She was used in two feature films, "The Bridges of Toko-Ri," starring William Holden, and "The Men of the Fighting Lady."

Q. Why is an orphanage in Shizuoka, Japan, named Oriskany Hall?

A. When the Oriskany's crew found out that the Catholic order of sisters operating the orphanage needed money to house another 100 orphans, the sailors donated $3,225.

Q. When was the Oriskany mothballed?

A. She was decommissioned in September, 1976 and put into mothballs at the Naval Shipyard, Bremerton, Wash.

Q. Where is the Oriskany's anchor?

A. On display in the Village of Oriskany's park.

Q. Who owns the anchor?

A. It is on indefinite loan from the U.S. Navy.

Q. How much does the anchor weigh?

A. The anchor weighs 15 tons, the chain weighs three tons.

Q. What else of military significance is on display in the park?

A. A Navy A-4 Skyhawk jet fighter.

Q. Why a Skyhawk?

A. Skyhawks once flew off the Oriskany.

HISTORY, HISTORY, HISTORY

CHAPTER   SIXTEEN

Q. Who was the first president of the Oneida County Historical Society?

A. Gov. Horatio Seymour, 1876-86.

Q. How was Utica's name chosen?

A. It was picked out of a hat.

Q. What were other names in the hat?

A. "Sconondoa," in honor of an Oneida Indian chief; "Washington," in honor of the president; and "Kent," after a place in England.

Q. Where has the Oneida County Historical Society called home?

A. The Munson-Williams Memorial Building, intersection of Elizabeth, Park and John streets; the basement at Fountain Elms, Genesee Street; and now at 1608 Genesee.

Q. What anniversary was celebrated by the Utica Public Library in 1993?

A. 100 years of service to the Utica area.

Q. What was the total amount of taxes levied on Utica residents in 1800?

A. $40.

Q. What taxpayer got hit hardest in 1800?

A. John Post, whose total tax bill was $2.

Q. Who is the City of Utica's official historian?

A. Judge John J. Walsh.

Q. Who raised the money to build the Oriskany Monument at the site of the Battle of Oriskany?

A. The Oneida County Historical Society.

Q. What was the hottest day in Utica's history?

A. July 9, 1936, when temperatures ranging from 104 to 120 were recorded in the city.

Q. What was "Moonlight Savings Time"?

A. To save money, Utica once had a street lighting contract which provided for the lights to be turned off when the moon was bright.

Q. What did Utica consist of in 1832, when it became a city?

A. Utica had 10 hardware stores, five bookstores, 17 shoe shops, nine bakeries, three banks, seven hat shops, five hairdressers, two paint stores, six jewelry stores, 15 churches, 28 inns, 43 lawyers, 32 doctors, and a population of 10,000.

Q. To what Utican did Robert Louis Stevenson dedicate a poem?

A. Mother Marianne, a Franciscan nun who worked in a leper colony in Hawaii in the late 1800s.

Q. Before joining the Franciscans, where did Mother Marianne live and what was her name?

A. Barbara Cope lived on Schuyler Street and for a short time in her early years worked in the Utica Steam Woolen Mill.

Q. How long did Mother Marianne live and work with the lepers and did she get the disease?

A. She spent 35 years in the leper colony and died in 1918 at age 80 without getting leprosy.

Q. Who donated the land on which the Utica Public Library now sits?

A. The Proctor family.

Q. What was Dunham Station?

A. A U.S. Post Office substation located on Genesee Street, next to the Fort Schuyler Club.

Q. Who was Dunham Station named after?

A. George Dunham, editor of The Utica Daily Press and first president of the Utica Chamber of Commerce.

TRANSPORTATION TIDBITS

| CHAPTER SEVENTEEN |

Q. What made the horse-drawn, street-car line that transported passengers up and down Utica's Genesee Street starting in 1863 so unique?

A. Only four other cities had street car lines - Boston, New York City, Philadelphia and New Orleans.

Q. What once had two shoeshine stands, three ticket windows, one information window, a bar and grill, 15 pay telephones, and a busy Western Union office?

A. Utica's Union Station.

Q. How many marble columns are in Union Station's waiting room?

A. 34.

Q. How high is Union Station's vaulted ceiling?

A. 47 feet.

Q. How many passenger benches are in Union Station's waiting room?

A. There are eight benches, each one almost half as long as the width of the room.

Q. What makes the passenger benches unusual?

A. They contain steam heating pipes and vents to warm the people sitting on them.

Q. How many square feet is Union Station's waiting room?

A. About 15,000 square feet.

Q. What decorates Union Station's outside front wall?

A. Three eagles on each side of a clock.

Q. What company made the Union Station clock?

A. The Self Windit Clock Company, New York City.

Q. The clock's minute hand and hour hand are how long?

A. Four feet and three feet.

Q. What city department once had offices in Union Station?

A. In 1915, the Utica Police Department had offices on the station's upper floor.

Q. What barber has been cutting hair at Union Station since 1947?

A. Dan Creaco.

Q. How many members of the armed services took advantage of the USO being at Union Station during World War II?

A. 233,000 military people stopped at the USO's rooms.

Q. When did Union Station open for business and what did it cost?

A. The $1 million station opened its doors in 1914.

Q. How did passengers once get from Union Station's waiting room to the track platforms?

A. By an underground tunnel.

Q. How did baggage once get to the trains?

A. Elevators from the underground tunnels lifted the bags to train side.

Q. How many Red Caps (baggage handlers) once worked at Union Station?

A. In 1948, there were 11 Red Caps.

Q. How much did Red Caps charge for their services?

A. The 1950's rate was 35 cents a bag.

Q. What was the Mohawk & Malone?

A. A railway that connected the Mohawk Valley with Lake Placid.

Q. Why does Genesee Street follow the route that it does?

A. It follows an Indian trail.

Q. What major mass transit event happened on May 12, 1941?

A. The last trolley car in Utica made its final run.

Q. Before the Oneida County Airport was built, what airport served Utica?

A. The Utica Municipal Airport, River Road, Marcy.

Q. What airlines served the Utica Municipal Airport?

A. American Airlines and Colonial Airways.

Q. In terms of transportation, what did Genesee, Lincoln, Blandina, Arthur, Neilson, Elm, and James streets have in common?

A. All were on trolley car routes.

Q. The Overland Mail Company, which was owned and operated by Utica's John Butterfield, went from where to where?

A. From Tipton, Missouri, to San Francisco, a 2,812-mile trip.

Q. What was the significance of Overland's operation?

A. For the first time, there was regularly scheduled service transporting people and mail to California.

Q. How long did it take an Overland Stage to go from Missouri to San Francisco?

A. 23 days.

Q. Who did Butterfield later go into business with?

A. Henry Wells and William Fargo of Wells Fargo Express Company fame.

Q. What new company, which is now known around the world, did the three men form?

A. American Express.

Q. Who was American Express Company's first president?

A. Utica's John Butterfield.

Q. What do Grey, Best Yet, Cornhill, Blue Line, Central, Uptown and Hinckley & Wurz have in common?

A. All were taxi companies that once operated in Utica.

Q. What was the cost of building Oneida County Airport?

A. $2,225,000.

Q. What airline first served Oneida County Airport?

A. Robinson Airlines, which made the first regularly scheduled commercial flight from the airport on Aug. 30, 1950.

Q. What airline did Robinson later become?

A. Mohawk Airlines.

Q. How long and wide is Oneida County Airport's runway 15-33?

A. 6,001 feet long and 150 feet wide.

Q. What are the dimensions of runway 9-27 at the county airport?

A. 5,400 feet by 150 feet.

Q. When did the state Thruway open?

A. 1955.

Q. Who started Utica's first stagecoach line?

A. Jason Parker operated a stagecoach line between Canajoharie and Whitestown, starting in 1794.

Q. How long did it take early 19th century travelers to go from Utica to Albany?

A. In 1811, Utica's Parker & Powell stagecoach company offered "one day service" to Albany, a feat which required eight changes of horses.

Q. What railroad invention did Utican Irvin Williams receive patents for in the mid-1800s?

A. He made the first practical locomotive headlight, and manufactured the oil lights in Utica until 1900, when electric headlights came into being.

Q. What was the speed limit on Utica streets in 1908?

A. 8 miles per hour.

Q. What was the Remington Standard and the Buckmobile?

A. Automobiles manufactured in Central New York around the turn of the century.

Q. What distinction is enjoyed by the Automobile Club of Utica?

A. In 1902, it was one of nine such clubs in the United States to gather in Chicago to form the American Automobile Association (AAA).

Q. Where in Utica were bodies for Lincoln, Cadillac and Studebaker automobiles once made?

A. In the early 1900s, the Willoughby Company built the bodies at its plant on Dwyer Avenue and Turner Street, near where CharlesTown is today.

Q. What did the 97-mile long Chenango Canal connect?

A. Utica and Binghamton.

Q. How many locks were on the Chenango Canal?
A. 116.

Q. Why was the canal important?
A. Coal from Pennsylvania could be cheaply transported to Utica's factories.

Q. What route did the Chenango Canal take through Utica?

A. It followed the approximate route of today's North-South Arterial.

Q. Utica was once a stop on what "railroad"?

A. The Underground Railroad, a clandestine network that transported runaway southern slaves to Canada.

Q. What ceremony took place in Rome on July 4, 1817, that led to one of the biggest transportation events in U.S. history?

A. The first shovel of earth was turned over for the building of the Erie Canal.

Q. When was the Erie Canal between Rome and Utica completed?

A. The 16-mile section opened to traffic in October 1819.

Q. What happened to the population of Oneida County as a result of the Erie Canal?

A. It spurred growth to the extent that Oneida County was second only to New York County in population in 1825.

Q. What size was the original Erie Canal?

A. 40 feet wide at the top, 28 feet wide at the bottom and four feet deep.

Q. How long was the Erie Canal?

A. It ran the width of the state, 363 miles from the Hudson River to Lake Erie.

Q. When was the entire Erie Canal completed?

A. 1825.

Q. What ceremony marked the opening of the Erie Canal?

A. A "wedding of the waters," which happened when a keg of water brought from Lake Erie was poured into the Atlantic Ocean.

Q. Where did the Erie Canal flow through Utica?

A. Along the present-day route of Oriskany Street.

Q. What important Erie Canal facility was across the street from where the Observer-Dispatch building stands today?

A. A weighlock building, where boats were weighed and tonnage recorded.

Q. What other canal structure was near the newspaper building?

A. The John Street Bridge, which spanned the Erie Canal.

Q. By what other name was the Erie Canal known?

A. Critics referred to it as "Clinton's Ditch," a reference to Gov. DeWitt Clinton, the driving force behind the canal.

THEN AND NOW

CHAPTER EIGHTEEN

Q. What was Lafayette Street originally called?

A. It was changed from Rome Street after the Marquis de Lafayette used the street to ride into Utica on a visit in 1825.

Q. What now occupies what was once the Utica City National Bank on the west side of Genesee Street, just north of Oriskany Street?

A. The former bank has been converted to an apartment building.

Q. What do Mechanics Hall, the old City Hall, and Elizabeth Street between Genesee and Charlotte streets have in common?

A. All were sites of the Utica Public Library before it moved to its present Genesee Street location.

Q. Gaffney Communications is in a building at 310 Main Street that once housed what business?

A. The Utica Daily Press.

Q. The parking lot on the east side of the Observer-Dispatch was once the site of what businesses?

A. Field & Start wholesale grocers, Utica Merchandise and Paper Co., and the Barbershop bar.

Q. Before moving to Bleecker Street and Third Avenue in 1975, where was the Central Fire Station located?

A. Built in 1911, it was at Elizabeth and Burnet streets, across from the Oneida County Court House.

Q. What was Lenox Avenue's original name?
A. West End Avenue.

Q. Prior to its Burrstone Road campus, where was Utica College located?

A. In buildings scattered around Oneida Square.

Q. What was once on the Rutger Street site now occupied by the Historical Park Apartments?

A. A New York State Armory.

Q. What were Utica Common Councilmen once called?

A. Aldermen.

Q. Before it was the Dave Hayes Appliance Center, what Genesee Street business occupied the building?

A. Shopper's City, a discount retail outlet.

Q. The parking lot next to the Sons of Italy on Bleecker Street once was the site of what business?

A. Tex's Bowling Alley.

Q. The Children's Museum, Main Street next to Union Station, was once the home of what business?

A. Hieber Dry Goods.

Q. What automobile dealer once occupied the building where Clemente Novelties now does business?

A. Ray Benson Chevrolet.

Q. Before Zip Codes, how was mail delivered in Utica?

A. The city was divided into four postal zones.

Q. The Oneida County Board of Legislators was once called what?

A. The Oneida County Board of Supervisors.

Q. Dapper Dan's Dry Cleaning, the circular building at Genesee Street and Auburn Avenue, was once used by what business?

A. The Homestead Savings and Loan Association.

Q. What business was once housed in the Tri-State Laundries building on Lincoln Avenue?

A. The Kleen-Maid Bakery.

Q. Griffiss Air Force Base originally had what name?

A. Rome Air Depot.

Q. What was Rome's original name?

A. Lynchville, named after its founder, Dominick Lynch.

Q. Where was the Salvation Army's facility located before it moved to Clinton Place?

A. Blandina Street, near Genesee.

Q. What charitable organization preceded the United Way?

A. The Community Chest.

Q. Before Chicago Pneumatic Tool Company was built, what occupied the site?

A. Utica Park, which had picnic grounds, athletic fields and rides, including a roller coaster.

Q. What purpose did Broadacres serve before being turned into a county nursing home?

A. It was a tuberculosis sanitarium.

Q. What was St. Anthony Street's original name?

A. Buffalo Street.

Q. Before 1908, when it was moved to its present location, where was the Oneida County Court House located?

A. The east side of John Street, between Elizabeth and Bleecker.

Q. Utica's police station, now on Oriskany Street, used to be located where?

A. It was behind the old City Hall on Genesee Street until 1934, when it was torn down and the property used as a parking lot for City Hall employees.

Q. Empire Bath and Kitchen, at State and Columbia streets, once housed what car dealer?

A. McRorie-Sautter Buick.

Q. What now occupies the site of the Royal Bowling Alley, northeast corner of Seymour Avenue and South Street?

A. A vacant lot.

Q. What company once did business in the building at Main and First, now occupied by the Trackside Tavern?

A. Utica Gear and Auto Parts.

Q. Where was Grant's Book Shop once located?

A. At Genesee and Hopper streets in a building now occupied by Key Bank.

Q. Before offices occupied the building on Genesee, corner of Dakin Street, what was housed there?

A. The Towne House Restaurant.

Q. Before Citibank was on the southwest side of the Busy Corner, what was there?

A. Wolfies Donuts.

Q. What used to be on the site of the shopping center at South and Mohawk streets?

A. Utica General Hospital.

Q. What was Sunset Avenue's original name?

A. Perkins Avenue, named after a family which owned much land in south Utica.

Q. Niagara Mohawk evolved from what company?

A. The Utica Gas and Electric Co.

Q. Where was the Christopher Columbus statue located before it was moved to the Memorial Parkway?

A. On Oriskany Street, across from the Observer-Dispatch.

Q. Before it became Noyes Street, what was its name?

A. Hickory Street.

Q. The Oneida County Jail is now located near the airport in Oriskany, but where in Utica was the lockup once located?

A. On Mohawk Street, near Eagle, and after that it was on Bleecker Street at the foot of Albany Street.

Q. Before moving to its present location at Genesee and Elizabeth streets in 1860, where was Grace Church located?

A. Corner of Columbia Street and Broadway.

Q. Where in Utica were horse races once held?

A. At the Utica Driving Park, now the site of Masonic Home.

NUMBERS, NAMES AND NUGGETS OF INFORMATION

| CHAPTER NINETEEN |

Q. How many fire hydrants are there in the city?

A. 1,749.

Q. How big is the city's water main system?

A. There are 218 miles of water mains running beneath city streets, and attached to the mains are 4,506 shut-off valves.

Q. How many requests for information did the Utica Public Library's Reference Department respond to in 1992?

A. 52,327.

Q. How many U.S. mail collection boxes are there in the city?

A. 257.

Q. What is Utica's official flower?

A. The peony, which was chosen by a city-wide vote in 1963.

Q. How many inches of snow fell during the Blizzard of '66?

A. Between Jan. 31 and Feb. 3, 1966, a total of 30 inches of snow fell on Utica.

Q. What material was used in the construction of the Baron von Steuben statue on the east side of Genesee Street and the Parkway?

A. The statue of the Revolutionary War hero was cast in bronze and is mounted on a granite pedestal.

Q. Why is there a statue of an eagle on the hill overlooking Utica in Roscoe Conkling Park?

A. The statue is in memory of Thomas Proctor who gave the park to the city and who once purchased a caged eagle for the sole purpose of setting it free.

Q. What type of penmanship was once taught to Utica school students?

A. Palmer Method.

Q. What penmanship exercises did Palmer Method students practice time after time?

A. Ovals and push-pulls.

Q. Who was the instructor who administered the Palmer Method program?

A. Miss Lucilla McCalmont.

Q. What personal connection did aviation legend Amelia Earhart have with this area?

A. Earhart's sister was a teacher in New Hartford's Country Day School and the aviatrix visited her there.

Q. What statue stands on the north side of the Utica Public Library?

A. George Washington.

Q. The statue is supposed to represent Washington at what age?

A. Age 44.

Q. Who was Arthur Hind and what made him famous?

A. He was a wealthy Utica industrialist and the owner of one of the world's best stamp collections, including the one-of-a-kind 1856 British Guiana one-cent magenta.

Q. Who did Hind have to outbid at an auction to get the stamp?

A. In 1922, Hind paid $34,000 for the stamp, which England's King George wanted for his collection.

Q. How much was Hind's collection worth?

A. In the 1920s, it was worth about $2 million.

Q. Who paid for the statue of Thomas R. Proctor, built in 1921 in Roscoe Conkling Park, just off the Parkway?

A. Most of the money was contributed by school children.

Q. What were the Blue Star, Bouse's, Master's, Squires and Shamrock?

A. Pool halls.

Q. What was the name of the world-famous botanist born in Sauquoit in 1810?

A. Asa Gray.

Q. How many tons of newsprint were recycled by the Oneida-Herkimer Solid Waste Authority in 1992?

A. 10,463 tons.

Q. How many tons of telephone books did the authority recycle?

A. 123 tons.

Q. How many licenses for various hunting and fishing sports were issued in 1992 in Oneida, Herkimer, Madison, Otsego and Lewis counties?

A. A total of 126,679 licenses.

Q. How many public school districts are in Oneida County?

A. There are 29 districts, which adds up to 108 schools.

Q. How many private or religious schools are there in Oneida County?

A. 30.

AfterWORDs

Q. How come you didn't list any trivia about the Boston Store, Proctor High School, or the Utica Zoo?

A. For the same reason the YMCA, Valley View Golf Course, Kennedy High School and hundreds of other great topics weren't mentioned - there wasn't enough room in a book that scratches just the surface.

Q. What if my favorite bit of trivia wasn't included in this book?

A. Don't worry. Information is now being gathered for "JOE KELLY'S GREATEST EVER LITTLE TRIVIA BOOK, VOLUME II" or *"I HAD TO WRITE ANOTHER TRIVIA BOOK BECAUSE THERE WASN'T ENOUGH ROOM FOR EVERYTHING IN THE FIRST ONE".*

Q. What if I have trivia to share?

A. Contact me. If the information is used in the next trivia book, you'll get credit - no money, mind you, but credit.

Q. When will the next trivia book be published?

A. Probably in 1995.

Q. Will you have any books out before then?

A. Yes, another book is scheduled for 1994.

Q. What will that book be about?

A. Maybe a book containing letters people have sent me and my responses, maybe a picture postcard tour book of Oneida County, maybe a - well, I'm not sure which book is next, but I am sure it will be out in 1994.

Q. Who will it be published by?

A. Good Times Publishing.

Q. If I have a book or a book idea, would Good Times be interested?

A. To find out, write to Good Times, P.O. Box 4545, Utica, NY 13504.

Q. If I like the book I just read, who should I tell?

A. Everybody, including total strangers you see shopping at the mall.

Q. What if I didn't like this crummy book?

A. My hope is that you don't get out and talk to people very often.

ABOUT THE AUTHOR

Joe Kelly was born in Utica, and attended Miller Street School, Conkling School, Utica Free Academy, Mohawk Valley Community College and Utica College. He was an assistant to Utica Mayor Michael Caruso, State Sen. James Donovan and since 1975 has worked at the Observer-Dispatch, starting as a reporter and later becoming the newspaper's first full-time columnist. He does a commentary heard twice daily on radio station WIBX.